Stage 1+
Decode and Develop
Liz Miles

Group/Guided Reading Notes

Contents

Introduction	2
Comprehension strategies	3
Vocabulary and phonic opportunities	4
Curriculum coverage chart	5

Hop! Hop! Pop!
Group or guided reading	8
Group and independent reading activities	9
Speaking, listening and drama activities	10
Writing activities	11

Catkin the Kitten
Group or guided reading	12
Group and independent reading activities	13
Speaking, listening and drama activities	14
Writing activities	15

In the Trolley
Group or guided reading	16
Group and independent reading activities	17
Speaking, listening and drama activities	18
Writing activities	18

The Trampoline
Group or guided reading	20
Group and independent reading activities	21
Speaking, listening and drama activities	22
Writing activities	23

The Enormous Crab
Group or guided reading	24
Group and independent reading activities	25
Speaking, listening and drama activities	26
Writing activities	27

The Caterpillar
Group or guided reading	28
Group and independent reading activities	29
Speaking, listening and drama activities	30
Writing activities	31

Introduction

Oxford Reading Tree stories at Stages 1–4 feature settings and situations most children will find familiar. The stories reflect the experiences of most 4–6 year-olds: having a bath, going to a party, having new shoes, getting into trouble. Children of this age will readily identify with the characters and situations. This also helps build comprehension.

Each *Decode and Develop* book tells a complete story, using natural language, with a greater number of phonically decodable words and a selection of high frequency words, all supported by funny and engaging pictures. The books offer plenty of scope for developing children's decoding and language comprehension skills. When used alongside your systematic phonic teaching they will help children put all their reading skills into practice in a highly motivating way.

Using the books

This booklet provides suggestions for using the books for guided, group and independent activities. The reading activities include ideas for developing children's *word recognition* **W** and *language comprehension* **C** skills. Within word recognition, there are ideas for helping children practise their phonic skills and knowledge, as well as helping them to tackle words which are not easy to decode phonically. The language comprehension ideas include suggestions for teaching the skills of prediction, questioning, clarifying, summarising and imagining in order to help children understand the text and the whole stories. Suggestions are also provided for speaking, listening, drama and writing activities.

Reading fluency

To support children in developing fluency in their reading, give them plenty of opportunities to revisit the stories. This includes:

- re-reading independently
- re-reading with a partner
- re-reading at home
- listening to audio versions of the story (e.g. Talking Stories)
- hearing the story read to them by others as they follow the printed text.

Re-reading and re-hearing helps children develop automatic word recognition and gives them models of fluent, expressive reading.

Comprehension strategies

Story	Comprehension strategy taught through these Group/Guided Reading Notes				
	Prediction	Questioning	Clarifying	Summarising	Imagining
Hop! Hop! Pop!	✓	✓	✓	✓	
Catkin the Kitten	✓	✓	✓	✓	
In the Trolley	✓	✓	✓	✓	✓
The Trampoline	✓		✓	✓	✓
The Enormous Crab	✓	✓	✓	✓	✓
The Caterpillar	✓	✓	✓	✓	

Vocabulary and phonic opportunities

Each story contains many decodable words, providing lots of opportunities to practise phonic and word recognition skills. This chart shows the tricky words used in each book. Most of these tricky words are common but do not conform to the phonic rules taught up to this point – children will need support to learn and recognise them. If children struggle with one of these words you can model how to read it.

Hop! Hop! Pop!	Tricky words	the go was Chip hopper Kipper hooray wins
Catkin the Kitten	Tricky words	the she was Wilma kitten lost basket
In the Trolley	Tricky words	the to see she went saw Kipper shopping trolley egg
The Trampoline	Tricky words	the down he she went oh Wilma Wilf trampoline
The Enormous Crab	Tricky words	the no will then me they enormous crab Chip held bucket out
The Caterpillar	Tricky words	the then see he we was caterpillar Kipper box leaves chrysalis butterfly

Curriculum coverage chart

	Speaking, listening, drama	Reading	Writing
Hop! Hop! Pop!			
PNS Literacy Framework (YF)	1.4, 2.3	**W** 5.1, 5.4 **C** 7.3	12
National Curriculum	Working towards Level 1		
Scotland: Curriculum for Excellence (P1)	Early level: LIT 0-02a/ENG 0-03a LIT 0-07a/LIT 0-15a/ENG 0-17a	Early level: LIT 0-01a/ LIT 0-11a/LIT 0-20a LIT 0-13a/LIT 0-21a LIT 0-19a	Early level: LIT 0-21b
N. Ireland (Foundation Stage)	Talking and listening: Attention and listening skills 2, 3; Phonological awareness 5; Social use of language 3, 4; Language and thinking 1–11, Extended vocabulary 1–3	Reading: 1–9	Writing: 1–6
Wales (Key Stage 1)	Range: 2b Skills: 2, 4, 5a Language: 2, 3	Range: 1, 3, 5a Skills: 1, 2a, b	Range: 2, 3 Skills: 1, 8b, e, 9 Language: 3
Catkin the Kitten			
PNS Literacy Framework (YF)	2.2, 3.2	**W** 5.4 **C** 7.3, 7.4	6.1, 9
National Curriculum	Working towards Level 1		
Scotland: Curriculum for Excellence (P1)	Early level: LIT 0-02a/ENG 0-03a LIT 0-07a/LIT 0-16a/ENG 0-17a	Early level: LIT 0-13a/ LIT 0-21a LIT 0-19a	Early level: ENG 0-12a/LIT 0-13a/LIT 0-21a LIT 0-26a
N. Ireland (Foundation Stage)	Talking and listening: Attention and listening skills 2, 3; Phonological awareness 5; Social use of language 3, 4; Language and thinking 1–11, Extended vocabulary 1–3	Reading: 1–9	Writing: 1–6
Wales (Key Stage 1)	Range: 1a, c Skills: 1, 2, 3, 5 Language: 2, 3	Range: 1, 3, 5a Skills: 1, 2a, b, 4	Range: 1, 3, 6 Skills: 8b, c, e

Curriculum coverage chart

	Speaking, listening, drama	Reading	Writing
In the Trolley			
PNS Literacy Framework (YF)	4.1	**W** 5.7, 5.10 **C** 7.1, 7.3	6.1, 9
National Curriculum	Working towards Level 1		
Scotland: Curriculum for Excellence (P1)	Early level: LIT 0-10a	Early level: LIT 0-13a/ LIT 0-21a LIT 0-14a	Early level: ENG 0-12a/LIT 0-13a/LIT 0-21a LIT 0-26a
N. Ireland (Foundation Stage)	Talking and listening: Attention and listening skills 2, 3; Phonological awareness 5; Social use of language 3, 4; Language and thinking 1–11, Extended vocabulary 1–3	Reading: 1–9	Writing: 1–6
Wales (Key Stage 1)	Range: 5 Skills: 1, 2, 3, 4 Language: 2	Range: 1, 3, 5a Skills: 1, 2a, b, 4	Range: 1, 2, 7 Skills: 8b, c, e, h
The Trampoline			
PNS Literacy Framework (YF)	2.2	**W** 5.2, 5.8 **C** 7.3	9.1, 12
National Curriculum	Working towards Level 1		
Scotland: Curriculum for Excellence (P1)	Early level: LIT 0-02a/ENG 0-03a	Early level: LIT 0-01a/ LIT 0-11a/LIT 0-20a LIT 0-13a/LIT 0-21a LIT 0-19a	Early level: LIT 0-26a LIT 0-21b
N. Ireland (Foundation Stage)	Talking and listening: Attention and listening skills 2, 3; Phonological awareness 5; Social use of language 3, 4; Language and thinking 1–11, Extended vocabulary 1–3	Reading: 1–9	Writing: 1–6
Wales (Key Stage 1)	Range: 1b Skills: 2, 4, 5a Language: 3b	Range: 1, 3, 5a Skills: 1, 2a, b,	Range: 3 Skills: 2, 8b, c, e, h

Curriculum coverage chart

	Speaking, listening, drama	Reading	Writing
The Enormous Crab			
PNS Literacy Framework (YF)	1.4, 4.1	**W** 5.1, 5.4, 5.5, 5.6 **C** 7.3	6.1, 9
National Curriculum	Working towards Level 1		
Scotland: Curriculum for Excellence (P1)	Early level: LIT 0-02a/ENG 0-03a LIT 0-10a	Early level: LIT 0-01a/ LIT 0-11a/LIT 0-20a LIT 0-13a/LIT 0-21a LIT 0-19a	Early level: ENG 0-12a/LIT 0-13a/LIT 0-21a LIT 0-26a
N. Ireland (Foundation Stage)	Talking and listening: Attention and listening skills 2, 3; Phonological awareness 5; Social use of language 3, 4; Language and thinking 1–11, Extended vocabulary 1–3	Reading: 1–9	Writing: 1–6
Wales (Key Stage 1)	Range: 5 Skills: 2, 4, 6a Language: 2	Range: 1, 3, 5a Skills: 1, 2a, b, 4	Range: 1, 2 Skills: 8b, c, d, e, 9
The Caterpillar			
PNS Literacy Framework (YF)	1.2, 1.4, 8.2	**W** 5.1, 5.4, 5.6 **C** 7.3, 8.2	10, 12
National Curriculum	Working towards Level 1		
Scotland: Curriculum for Excellence (P1)	Early level: LIT 0-01c LIT 0-02a/ENG 0-03a	Early level: LIT 0-01a/ LIT 0-11a/LIT 0-20a LIT 0-13a/LIT 0-21a LIT 0-19a	Early level: LIT 0-26a LIT 0-21b
N. Ireland (Foundation Stage)	Talking and listening: Attention and listening skills 2, 3; Phonological awareness 5; Social use of language 3, 4; Language and thinking 1–11, Extended vocabulary 1–3	Reading: 1–9	Writing: 1–6
Wales (Key Stage 1)	Range: 1a Skills: 1, 2, 3 Language: 2, 3d	Range: 1, 3, 5a Skills: 1, 2a, b	Range: 1, 3 Skills: 8b, c, 9

Key

C = Language comprehension   Y = Year   P = Primary
W = Word recognition   F = Foundation/reception

In the designations such as 5.2, the first number represents the strand and the second number the individual objective

Hop! Hop! Pop!

> **C** = Language comprehension   **R, AF** = QCA reading assessment focus
> **W** = Word recognition   **W, AF** = QCA writing assessment focus

Group or guided reading

Introducing the book

C *(Questioning)* Read the title to the children, pointing to the words. Look at the cover picture. Ask the children: *Who are the children in the picture? What are they doing?*

C *(Clarifying)* Talk about the word 'Pop'. Ask: *What goes 'pop'?* Discuss how balloons can go pop and how hoppers are like balloons.

C *(Prediction)* Look at page 5. Ask: *Who do you think will win this race? Do you think Dad will be fast on a hopper?*

- Encourage the children to talk about their own experiences of things that have gone 'pop'.

Strategy check

Do the children understand that the text in speech bubbles is spoken text?

Independent reading

- Look at the cover again. Ask the children to read the title and then the story aloud. Praise them while they read, and prompt as necessary.
- Encourage the children to read the speech bubbles with expression.

C *(Clarifying)* On page 7, ask: *What has happened to Dad's hopper?*

Assessment Check that children:

- *(R, AF1)* use a range of phonic knowledge to sound out and blend the phonemes

- *(R, AF4)* understand that an exclamation mark means the sentence should be read in a lively, exciting way.

Returning to the text

C *(Summarising)* Ask the children to re-tell the story in their own words.

W On page 1, point to 'Biff' and ask them to sound out the letters. Ask: *Which two letters make one sound?* (ff) Point to 'hoppers'. Can they find two letters that make one sound in this word? (pp)

Group and independent reading activities

Objective Show an understanding of the elements of stories, such as main character, sequence of events, and openings (7.3).

C *(Questioning, Clarifying)* Ask the children the following questions:

Page 1: *Who are racing on the hoppers?*

Page 3: *Who wins the race?*

Pages 4–5: *Who rides on the red hopper? Why didn't Kipper get on the red hopper?*

Page 8: *Why is everyone laughing? How does Dad feel?*

Assessment *(R, AF2)* Do the children refer to the text as well as the pictures when answering the questions?

Objective Explore and experiment with sounds, words and texts (5.1).

W **You will need** letter cards for m, t, h, s, c, op.

- Write 'pop' on the board and encourage the children to sound out the letters.
- Ask them to use the letter cards to make words that rhyme with 'pop'.

Assessment *(R, AF1)* Do the children check their words to make sure they make sense?

Hop! Hop! Pop!

Objective Hear and say sounds in words in the order in which they occur (5.4).

- **(W)** Write the word 'hop' on the board. Model how to mark each letter sound with a counter or mark, as you sound out the word.
- Ask children to do the same with other words from the book, such as 'pop', 'got', 'in', 'it', and 'Biff'.
- Point to words randomly in the book and ask the children to count the sounds.

Assessment *(R, AF1)* Do the children understand that ff in 'Biff' is one sound?

Speaking, listening and drama activities

Objective Speak clearly and audibly with confidence and control and show awareness of the listener (1.4). Extend their vocabulary, exploring the meanings and sounds of new words (2.3).

- Sit in a circle with the children and explain you are going to have a sound quiz. Ask the children: *What makes this sound – 'buzz'?* Encourage suggestions then tell the children what you were thinking of, e.g. a bee, or a fly.
- Encourage children to take turns asking the question, *What makes this sound … ?* Encourage each child to speak loudly so that everyone can hear what they say.
- The children discuss possible answers, then the questioner says what they were thinking of.
- Continue around the group.

Writing activities

Objective Use a pencil and hold it effectively to form recognisable letters, most of which are correctly formed (12).

You will need paper and a variety of pencils, crayons and coloured pencils.

- Ask the children to choose a sound, draw the object that makes the sound, then write the sound it makes as a speech bubble.
- Remind them of some of the simple sound words discussed in the speaking and listening activity.
- Prompt with spellings if necessary, encouraging children to sound out the letters to check their spelling afterwards.

Assessment *(W, AF8)* Are the children able to spell the words correctly?

Catkin the Kitten

> **C** = Language comprehension   **R, AF** = QCA reading assessment focus
> **W** = Word recognition   **W, AF** = QCA writing assessment focus

Group or guided reading

Introducing the book

C *(Questioning)* Read the title to the children, pointing to the words. Look at the cover picture. Ask the children: *Who are the children in the picture? What are they doing?*

W Talk about the word 'Catkin'. Ask: *Why is it a good name for a cat?* Point out the smaller word 'Cat' within 'Catkin'.

C *(Prediction)* Look at page 3 and read it together. Ask: *Where do you think Catkin has gone?*

- Encourage the children to talk about their own experiences of pets.

Strategy check

Remind the children to read from left to right and to sound out the words.

Independent reading

- Look at the cover again. Ask the children to read the title and then the story aloud. Praise them while they read, and prompt as necessary.
- Encourage the children to read the longer words, sounding out and blending the phonemes.

C *(Clarifying)* On page 8, ask: *Why is Wilma putting a bell on Catkin?*

Assessment Check that children:

- *(R, AF1)* use phonic knowledge to sound out words that are not familiar to them
- *(R, AF2)* use comprehension skills to work out what is happening.

Returning to the text

C *(Summarising)* Ask the children to re-tell the story in their own words.

W On page 2, point to 'off' and ask them to sound out the letters. Ask: *Which two letters make one sound?* (ff) Repeat for 'kitten' on page 1.

Group and independent reading activities

Objective Show an understanding of the elements of stories, such as main character, sequence of events, and openings (7.3).

C *(Questioning, Clarifying)* Ask the children the following questions:

Page 2: *Why don't the children see where Catkin runs to?*

Pages 4–6: *Which three places did the children look before they found Catkin?* (bed, bin, bag)

Page 7: *Where did the children find Catkin?*

- *Is Catkin a good name for a kitten? Why? What is a catkin?* (downy-looking tree bud)

Assessment *(R, AF2)* Do the children refer to the text as well as the pictures when answering the questions?

Objective Hear and say sounds in words in the order in which they occur (5.4).

W Point to the title. Check the children understand that **tt** in 'kitten' makes one /t/ sound.

- Ask the children to find more words with the /t/ sound throughout the book.
- Encourage the children to list the words they find, and to underline the /t/ sounds in pencil.

Assessment *(R, AF9)* Do the children spot the /t/ sound in 'lost'?

Objective Retell narratives in the correct sequence, drawing on the language patterns of the stories (7.4).

G Ask the children to re-tell the story to you. Hide the text on each page but encourage the children to use each picture as a prompt.
- After each page, reveal the text and read it together.
- Point to words randomly in the book and ask the children to count the sounds.

Assessment *(R, AF2)* Do the children use vocabulary from the story?

Speaking, listening and drama activities

Objective Sustain attentive listening, responding to what they have heard by relevant comments, questions and actions (2.2). Use talk to organise, sequence and clarify thinking, ideas, feelings and events (3.2).

- Encourage the children to think of a time when they could not find something, e.g. a pet, a book, a bag.
- Encourage children to take turns to tell their story of what they lost, where they looked and where they found it.
- After each story has been told, encourage the listeners to ask questions, about the event or the object.
- Continue around the group.

Writing activities

Objective Attempt writing for various purposes (9). Use phonic knowledge to write simple regular words and make phonetically plausible attempts at more complex words (6.1).

- Tell the children that they are going to write their own story about Biff and an animal that she loses.
- Write sentences from the story with blanks for the children to fill in:

    Biff had _____ .

    It was not _____ .

    It was not _____ .

    It was not _____ .

    But it was _____ .

- Write the story as a class, with volunteers writing the text to fill the gaps after class discussion.

Assessment *(W, AF7)* Do the children choose appropriate vocabulary that follows the pattern of the story?

In the Trolley

> **C** = Language comprehension   **R, AF** = QCA reading assessment focus
> **W** = Word recognition   **W, AF** = QCA writing assessment focus

Group or guided reading

Introducing the book

- **C** *(Questioning)* Read the title to the children. Look at the cover picture. Ask the children: *Who is the child in the picture? What might he be doing?*
- **C** *(Clarifying)* Turn to the back cover and read the blurb. Talk about where they might have gone shopping.
- **C** *(Prediction)* Look at page 5. Ask: *Who do you think the egg is for?*
- Encourage the children to talk about their own experiences of shopping in supermarkets and the things they are allowed to put in the trolley.

Strategy check

Do the children attempt to read unfamiliar words by sounding out and blending?

Independent reading

- Look at the cover again. Ask the children to read the title and then the story aloud. Praise them while they read, and prompt as necessary. Remind them how two of the same letters together makes one sound. (e.g. ll in 'trolley')
- **C** *(Questioning)* On page 7, ask: *Did Mum want to buy the egg? Who wanted the egg, Mum or Kipper?*
- **C** *(Clarifying, Imagining)* On page 8, ask: *Did Mum buy a chocolate egg? Who was it for?*

Assessment Check that children:
- *(R, AF1)* use phonic knowledge to sound out words that are not familiar to them
- *(R, AF2)* use comprehension skills to work out what is happening.

Returning to the text

C *(Summarising)* Ask the children to re-tell the story in their own words.

W On page 8, point to 'back' and explain that the two letters **ck** make one /c/ sound.

Group and independent reading activities

Objective Show an understanding of the elements of stories, such as main character, sequence of events, and openings (7.3).

C *(Questioning, Clarifying, Imagining)* Ask the children the following questions:

Page 3: *What is Kipper thinking here?*

Pages 3–4, 6: *Can you find three things that Mum put in the trolley?*

Page 5: *What did Kipper put in the trolley?*

Page 8: *How do you think Kipper feels? What is he thinking?*

Assessment *(R, AF2)* Do the children refer to the text as well as the pictures when answering the questions?

Objective Read some high frequency words (5.7).

W Point to high frequency words in the book at random (and, Mum, got, put, in, big, not, had, back).

- Ask the children to see how quickly they can read the words.
- Return to any words the children had difficulty with.

Assessment *(R, AF1)* Do the children recognise the digraph **ck** in 'back'?

Objective Know that print carries meaning and, in English, is read from left to right (7.1). Read texts compatible with their phonic knowledge and skills (5.10).

Ⓦ You will need two sets of word cards, each to make up a sentence from the book, e.g. 'Mum put cans in the trolley.' 'Mum did not see the big egg.'

- Ask the children to re-order the words to make a sentence. Repeat with the next set.
- Encourage them to find the sentence in the book to check their sentence is correct.

Assessment *(R, AF4)* Does the children's ordering of the words make grammatical sense?

Speaking, listening and drama activities

Objective Use language to imagine and recreate roles and experiences (4.1).

- Role-play Mum and encourage the children to ask you questions about the shopping trip.
- Afterwards, encourage a child to role-play Kipper, and the other children to ask Kipper about the shopping trip and the big chocolate egg.
- Encourage other children to role-play Mum and repeat.

Writing activities

Objective Attempt writing for various purposes (9). Use phonic knowledge to write simple regular words and make phonetically plausible attempts at more complex words (6.1).

- Tell the children that they are going to write a shopping list for Mum.

- Ask for ideas and scribe some items on the board, asking the children to help you spell the words correctly.
- Ask volunteers to add items that Kipper might want.
- Children could write out their own lists independently under the heading 'Shopping list'.

Assessment   *(W, AF7)* Do the children choose appropriate vocabulary and include words from the story?

(W, AF1) Do the children's choice of items for Mum and Kipper show an understanding of their characters?

The Trampoline

> **C** = Language comprehension   **R, AF** = QCA reading assessment focus
> **W** = Word recognition   **W, AF** = QCA writing assessment focus

Group or guided reading

Introducing the book

C *(Clarifying)* Read the title to the children, pointing to the words. Ask the children: *What is a trampoline?*

W Ask the children what the first sound is in 'trampoline'. Can they sound out the second sound and blend them together?

- Encourage the children to talk about their own experiences of trampolines, or other toys they can bounce on.

C *(Prediction)* Read the back cover blurb. Ask: *What do you think will happen in the story?*

Strategy check

Remind the children to read from left to right and to sound out the words.

Independent reading

- Look at the cover again. Encourage the children to sound out the first letters of 'Trampoline' again, then help with the rest of the word as necessary. Praise them while they read the rest of the book, prompting as necessary.

- Encourage the children to read difficult words, and to sound out and blend the phonemes.

C *(Prediction)* On page 7, ask: *What do you think has happened to Dad?*

Assessment Check that children:

- *(R, AF1)* use phonic knowledge to sound out words that are not familiar to them
- *(R, AF2)* use comprehension skills to work out what is happening.

Returning to the text

C *(Summarising)* Ask the children to re-tell the story in their own words.

W Ask the children to find 'up' each time it occurs in the story. Ask: *What letter sound does 'up' begin with?*

Group and independent reading activities

Objective Show an understanding of the elements of stories, such as main character, sequence of events, and openings (7.3).

C *(Questioning, Clarifying, Imagining)* Ask the children the following questions:

Page 2: *Why does Dad put a net up? What might happen if there wasn't a net?*

Page 3: Talk about opposites. Point to 'up' and ask: *Which word is the opposite of 'up'?*

Page 8: *How did Dad end up in a tree? How do you think he will get down?*

Assessment *(R, AF2)* Do the children refer to the text as well as the pictures when answering the questions?

Objective Use phonic knowledge to write simple regular words and make phonetically plausible attempts at more complex words (5.8).

W Write the following incomplete sentence from the book: 'Dad put the net ___ .'

- Ask the children for the missing word and to sound out the letters to help you spell 'up'.

The Trampoline

- Write the following incomplete sentence on the board: 'Wilma went up and ___ .' Prompt the missing word by saying it is the opposite of 'up'. Ask volunteers to help you spell 'down'. Repeat with other 'up' and 'down' sentences.

Assessment *(R, AF8)* Do the children use phonic knowledge to attempt their spelling of the missing words?

Objective Link sounds to letters, naming and sounding the letters of the alphabet (5.2).

(W) You will need word cards for: Mum, Dad, Wilf, up, down, she.

- Ask the children to identify the first letter sound of each word, and then to put the words in alphabetical order.
- If necessary, demonstrate with the words 'got' and 'net' first.

Assessment *(R, AF4)* Do the children understand the concept of organising words in alphabetical order?

Speaking, listening and drama activities

Objective Sustain attentive listening, responding to what they have heard by relevant comments, questions and actions (2.2).

- With the children in a circle, ask each in turn to say an 'up' and then a 'down' sentence.
- Begin by saying: *'I went up the hill ... then I went down the hill'.*
- Encourage and prompt children with ideas if necessary.
- Continue around the group.

Writing activities

Objective Attempt writing for various purposes (9). Use a pencil and hold it effectively to form recognisable letters, most of which are correctly formed (12).

- **You will need** reusable sticky labels and a list of words on the board written in speech bubbles: 'I go up ...; I go down; I will put the net up; Help!'
- Discuss the speech bubble on page 8. Explain that they are going to write speech bubbles for other pages.
- Encourage the children to choose a picture for one of the captions on the board and write it on the sticky label as a speech bubble.

Assessment *(W, AF7)* Do the children choose appropriate characters and pictures for the speech bubbles?

The Enormous Crab

> **C** = Language comprehension   **R, AF** = QCA reading assessment focus
> **W** = Word recognition   **W, AF** = QCA writing assessment focus

Group or guided reading

Introducing the book

- **C** *(Questioning, Imagining)* Read the title to the children. Look at the cover picture. Ask the children: *What do you think they are looking at? What are they thinking or saying?*
- **C** *(Clarifying, Imagining)* Ask: *What does enormous mean?* Look through the rest of the book and identify the biggest crab. Ask: *Would you like to hold this crab? Do you think it might nip you?*
- **C** *(Prediction)* Return to the cover and ask: *What do you think might happen in this story?*
- Encourage the children to talk about their own experiences of crabs or other seaside creatures.

Strategy check

Remind the children to sound out letters from left to right to blend words.

Independent reading

- Look at the cover again. Point to 'Enormous' and ask the children to attempt to sound out the letters left to right, to help you read the word. Show how splitting up a long word helps us to read it (write on the board 'E–norm–ous').
- **C** *(Clarifying)* Encourage the children to read the speech bubbles with expression.

(C) *(Prediction)* On page 7, ask: *Did the crab nip Dad?*

Assessment Check that children:

- *(R, AF1)* use a range of phonic knowledge to sound out and blend the phonemes
- *(R, AF4)* recognise the question marks and read the text as questions to be answered.

Returning to the text

(C) *(Summarising)* Ask the children to re-tell the story in their own words.

(W) On page 2, point to 'bucket' and ask the children to sound out the letters. Ask: *Which two letters make one sound?* (ck)

Group and independent reading activities

Objective Show an understanding of the elements of stories, such as main character, sequence of events, and openings (7.3).

(C) *(Questioning, Clarifying)* Hold a quiz and see who can find the answer to these questions first:

Page 4: *Who got the enormous crab?*

Page 5: *Who took the crab out of the net?*

Page 7: *Did the enormous crab nip Dad?*

Assessment *(R, AF2)* Do the children refer to the text as well as the pictures when answering the questions?

Objective Explore and experiment with sounds, words and texts (5.1). Recognise common digraphs (5.6).

(W) You will need letter cards for ck, s, b, u, e, t, o, a, p, r, m.

- Write the words 'bucket' and 'back' on the board. Ask: *How many letters are in each word and how many sounds?* ('bucket' 6, 5; 'back' 4, 3) Identify the digraph **ck** which makes one /c/ sound.

- Tell the children to try to make more 'ck' words using the letter cards. How many words can they make? (e.g. bucket, sock, back, pack, rock, rack)

Assessment *(R, AF1)* Do the children check their words and make sure they make sense? *(W, AF8)* Do the children use correct spelling?

Objective Hear and say sounds in words in the order in which they occur (5.4). Read simple words by sounding out and blending the phonemes all through the word from left to right (5.5).

- **(W)** Write 'crab' on the board and ask the children to sound out the word. Ask: *How do we change this to make more than one crab?* Add an 's' and ask the children to sound out the new word.
- Repeat with other words from the book: lot, lots; bucket, buckets; dad, dads.

Assessment *(R, AF1)* Do the children sound out all the letters from left to right?

Speaking, listening and drama activities

Objective Speak clearly and audibly with confidence and control and show awareness of the listener (1.4). Use language to imagine and recreate roles and experiences (4.1).

- **You will need** a selection of different-sized cardboard crabs in a bucket. Attach a string to each one.
- The children play in role as Chip, Biff, Kipper and Dad and take turns to pull out a crab. The group discusses each crab as it is 'caught', e.g. *Will it nip? It is enormous!*
- Encourage the children to play in role and use language from the book. Afterwards, ask: *Who got the enormous crab?* Ensure their answer uses the character's name, not the child's.

Writing activities

Objective Use phonic knowledge to write simple regular words and make phonetically plausible attempts at more complex words (6.1). Attempt writing for various purposes (9).

- **You will need** paper and a variety of pencils, crayons and coloured pencils.
- Look at and discuss the main parts of the cover and list them on the board with the children: title, picture, blurb (what the story is about).
- Talk about and write some alternative blurbs on the board, asking the children to help you spell words correctly.
- Ask the children to design their own cover for the book. Encourage them to write back cover blurb, too.

Assessment *(W, AF2)* Can the children write back cover blurb that makes sense?
(W, AF8) Do the children spell 'Enormous' correctly?

The Caterpillar

> **C** = Language comprehension   **R, AF** = QCA reading assessment focus
> **W** = Word recognition   **W, AF** = QCA writing assessment focus

Group or guided reading

Introducing the book

C *(Questioning)* Read the title to the children, pointing to the words. Look at the cover picture. Ask the children: *Who is the child? What is he holding?*

C *(Prediction)* Ask: *What do you think the story is about?* Turn to the back cover and read the blurb. Ask: *What do you think Kipper will do with the caterpillar?*

C *(Clarifying)* Look at and read pages 4–5. Ask: *What has happened to the caterpillar?*

● Talk about the way in which a caterpillar changes into a chrysalis, then a butterfly. Show pictures from a non-fiction book if necessary.

Strategy check

Do the children attempt to read unfamiliar words using phonic knowledge and sounding out the letters from left to right?

Independent reading

● Look at the cover again. Ask the children to read the title and then the story aloud. Praise them while they read, and prompt as necessary.

C *(Clarifying)* Encourage the children to explain what has happened at the end of each page, and to explain what the picture shows.

C *(Questioning, Clarifying)* On page 8, ask: *What has happened to the caterpillar?*

Assessment Check that children:
- *(R, AF1)* use a range of phonic knowledge to sound out and blend the phonemes
- *(R, AF3)* understand the stages of change for the caterpillar.

Returning to the text

C *(Summarising)* Ask the children to re-tell the story in their own words.

W Look at the cover and ask the children to help you read 'caterpillar'. Encourage them to split the word into parts, left to right, to make it easier to sound and blend (cat–er–pill–ar).

Group and independent reading activities

Objective Show an understanding of the elements of stories, such as main character, sequence of events, and openings (7.3, 8.2).

C *(Questioning, Clarifying)* Ask the children the following questions:

Page 2: *Where did Kipper put the caterpillar?*

Pages 4–5: *What did the caterpillar change into?*

Page 8: *What did the chrysalis change into?*

Assessment *(R, AF2)* Do the children refer to the text as well as the pictures when answering the questions? *(R, AF3)* Do they work out that the caterpillar eventually becomes a butterfly?

Objective Explore and experiment with sounds, words and texts (5.1).

W **You will need** word cards for: can, had, caterpillar, Kipper, chrysalis.

- Ask the children to find two words which contain the /a/ sound. Repeat for /i/, /c/ and /p/ sounds.

Assessment *(R, AF1)* Do the children remember how to sound out chrysalis?

Objective Hear and say sounds in words in the order in which they occur (5.4). Recognise common digraphs (5.6).

(W) Write the word 'caterpillar' on the board. Model how to mark each letter sound with a counter or mark, as you sound out the word.

- Ask children to attempt the same with other challenging words from the book, such as 'leaves', 'chrysalis', 'Kipper' and 'butterfly'.
- Point to words randomly in the book and ask the children to count the sounds.

Assessment (R, AF1) Do the children attempt to sound out and blend the longer words in sections?

Speaking, listening and drama activities

Objective Use talk to organise, sequence and clarify thinking, ideas, feelings and events (1.2). Speak clearly and audibly with confidence and control and show awareness of the listener (1.4). Show an understanding of the elements of stories such as sequence of events (8.2).

- Turn to page 4. Together look at the word 'Then' and discuss how this shows us the passing of time and the order in which things happen. Talk about this word and think of other words which tell us when things happen in a story (e.g. first, next, finally, afterwards, later).
- Encourage children to take turns to re-tell the story using one of these words at the start of their sentence.
- Prompt as necessary.

Writing activities

Objective Attempt writing for various purposes (10). Use a pencil and hold it effectively to form recognisable letters, most of which are correctly formed (12).

You will need paper and a variety of pencils, crayons and coloured pencils.

- Ask the children to show the sequence of changes from caterpillar to chrysalis to butterfly using drawings, labels and arrows. Encourage the children to use the story to help them remember the sequence.
- Remind them to take care over their spelling.
- Encourage each child to sound out the letters to check their spelling afterwards.

Assessment *(W, AF8)* Do the children make a logical attempt at spelling 'chrysalis'?

INSPIRATIONAL SUPPORT FOR TEACHERS
For free professional development videos from leading experts, plus other resources and free eBooks, please go to
www.oxfordprimary.co.uk

HELPING YOU ENGAGE PARENTS
We have researched the most common concerns and worries parents have about their children's literacy and provide answers and support in
www.oxfordowl.co.uk
This site contains advice on how to share a book, how to pronounce pure sounds, how to encourage boys' reading, and much more. We hope you will find the site useful and recommend it to your parents.

OXFORD
UNIVERSITY PRESS

Great Clarendon Street, Oxford OX2 6DP

Oxford University Press is a department of the University of Oxford. It furthers the University's objective of excellence in research, scholarship, and education by publishing worldwide in

Oxford New York
Auckland Cape Town Dar es Salaam Hong Kong Karachi
Kuala Lumpur Madrid Melbourne Mexico City Nairobi
New Delhi Shanghai Taipei Toronto

With offices in

Argentina Austria Brazil Chile Czech Republic France
Greece Guatemala Hungary Italy Japan Poland
Portugal Singapore South Korea Switzerland
Thailand Turkey Ukraine Vietnam

Oxford is a registered trade mark of Oxford University Press in the UK and in certain other countries

Text © Oxford University Press 2011

Written by Liz Miles, based on the original characters created by Roderick Hunt and Alex Brychta.

The moral rights of the author have been asserted

Database right Oxford University Press (maker)

First published 2011

All rights reserved. No part of this publication may be reproduced, stored in a retrieval system, or transmitted, in any form or by any means, without the prior permission in writing of Oxford University Press, or as expressly permitted by law, or under terms agreed with the appropriate reprographics rights organization. Enquiries concerning reproduction outside the scope of the above should be sent to the Rights Department, Oxford University Press, at the address above

You must not circulate this book in any other binding or cover and you must impose this same condition on any acquirer

British Library Cataloguing in Publication Data

Data available

Cover illustrations Alex Brychta and Nick Schon, based on the original characters created by Roderick Hunt and Alex Brychta

ISBN: 978-0-19-848384-7

10 9 8 7 6 5 4 3 2

Page make-up by Thomson Digital

Printed in China by Imago

Paper used in the production of this book is a natural, recyclable product made from wood grown in sustainable forests. The manufacturing process conforms to the environmental regulations of the country of origin.